LIFE IN
Estuaries

BY LAUREN COSS

The Child's World®

Published by The Child's World®
1980 Lookout Drive • Mankato, MN 56003-1705
800-599-READ • www.childsworld.com

Acknowledgments
The Child's World®: Mary Berendes, Publishing Director
Red Line Editorial: Editorial direction
The Design Lab: Design
Amnet: Production

Design Elements: Wild At Art/Shutterstock Images; Eric Isselee/
Shutterstock Images; Alexander Raths/Shutterstock Images

Photographs ©: Lone Wolf Photos/Shutterstock Images, cover
(center), 1 (center); Wild At Art/Shutterstock Images, cover;
Eric Isselee/Shutterstock Images, cover; Alexander Raths/
Shutterstock Images, cover; Shutterstock Images, 4–5, 6,
14, 17, 21, 21 (left); Tatiana Popova/Shutterstock Images,
8; Denton Rumsey/Shutterstock Images, 11; Ethan Daniels/
Shutterstock Images, 13; BD Digital Images/Shutterstock Images;
MountainHardcore/Shutterstock Images, 21 (middle); Shane
Gross/Shutterstock Images, 21 (right)

ISBN 9781626872943
LCCN 2014930648

Printed in the United States of America
Mankato, MN
July, 2014
PA02218

ABOUT THE AUTHOR

Lauren Coss is a writer and editor who lives in Minnesota. Her favorite estuary animal is the fiddler crab.

CONTENTS

Welcome to an Estuary

It is low tide at the estuary. Fiddler crabs scurry out of their holes. They scoot across the mud. The crabs look for tiny plants and animals to eat. *Squawk!* White seagulls call in the air. Spiky green marsh grasses wave in the breeze. Do you smell

rotten eggs? That is the smell of dead plants and animals.

This estuary is a water biome. A biome is a place in nature that supports certain types of life. An estuary is a body of water where salt water and freshwater mix. Estuaries are common along coasts around the world. Let's explore the estuary biome!

Fiddler crabs emerge from the sand in low tide.

What Is an Estuary?

Estuaries are found on the very edges of oceans. Here rivers and streams run into the sea. Freshwater mixes with salty seawater. The mixed water is called **brackish** water.

The Tairua River estuary is in New Zealand.

Estuaries are always changing. Sometimes the water is very salty. Sometimes the water is mostly freshwater. It has very little salt. The water depth also changes. This is because of tides. Water levels may be very low at low tide. Water levels are higher and saltier during high tide. Estuary plants and animals **adapt** to the changing water.

Many different **habitats** are in estuaries. They can include open water and salt marshes. Estuaries also have muddy flatlands and mangrove forests. Swamps and oyster reefs are also in estuaries. These habitats are home to many plants and animals.

An Estuary Forms

There are four different types of estuaries. Coastal plain estuaries form when the sea level rises.

The Geiranger fjord is off Norway's coast.

The ocean floods into a river delta. The seawater fills part of the river valley. The Chesapeake Bay in Maryland is a coastal plain estuary.

You may have visited an estuary before. Estuaries are also called sounds, bays, lagoons, or harbors.

Some estuaries have islands nearby. These islands formed from sand bars offshore. The islands trap freshwater flowing into the ocean. This makes a bar built estuary. Bar built estuaries are common along the Gulf of Mexico.

Tectonic estuaries form when land folds or splits apart. An earthquake might break land off from a coast. Seawater then flows into the opening created. The seawater mixes with freshwater. San Francisco Bay is a tectonic estuary. It is off the coast of California.

Fjords are common along the coasts of Norway, Alaska, and Canada. Glaciers carved valleys into coastal lands. These valleys, called fjords, are deep and narrow. Over time the glaciers melted. Then the valleys filled with seawater. The narrow fjord walls also trap freshwater. There it mixes with salty seawater.

A Salt Marsh

Salt marshes can be found in cooler water. These wetlands are filled with different grasses. Small streams run through to the coast. Seawater rushes up the streams when the tide comes in. Parts of the marsh are always underwater. Other parts only flood during high tides and storms.

Salt marsh grasses are built for their changing habitat. Cordgrass has sturdy roots. The roots dig deep into the muddy marsh floor. This plant can stay rooted in the ground as water rushes in and out. The roots also trap mud and sand.

Different animals live in salt marshes. Deer and other large animals eat the grasses. Crabs search for food during low tide. Hungry animals also search for **prey**. Raccoons, muskrats, and otters are common. Birds fly in to look for small fish and **crustaceans**. Some birds build nests in the grass.

In Alaska, grizzly bears visit salt marshes. These huge **predators** look for their prey. The bears dig in the mud. They find fat worms and juicy clams.

A Great Blue Heron watches the water for fish in a salt marsh.

The Mangrove Forest

Mangrove forests grow in warm, shallow salt water. The trees' roots are very tall. Mangroves look a little like they are on stilts. The roots may be underwater during high tide. Other times they are dry.

Mangrove forests burst with life. Monkeys, lizards, and birds move about the branches. Algae grow on the tree roots. Snails graze on the algae. Oysters, barnacles, and other **mollusks** attach to the roots. Mammals, fish, and birds feed on these animals.

Fish swim between mangrove roots. The waters of the mangrove forest are very calm. Fish lay their eggs there. Baby fish hide between the roots to stay safe. Plenty of bigger fish patrol the roots for smaller fish.

Mangrove tree roots reach underwater during high tide.

Into the Mud

Mudflats are covered with water during high tide. But they are bare at low tide. The muddy floor of an estuary is crawling with life. It is home to the flounder

The Leopard Flounder hides on an estuary's floor.

fish. This very flat fish is a clever hunter. It lies on its side. Then it digs into the muddy bottom. The fish waits for prey to swim past. Both a flounder's eyes are on one side of its head. It spots its prey while lying in the mud.

Other animals dig deeper into the mud. Clams use a **siphon** to breathe and eat. The siphon is part of a clam's body. The clam pushes the siphon up through the mud. The siphon pulls food from the water. It also brings air to the clam below.

Worms are another common mudflat creature. Ribbon worms are very thin. But they can grow to be more than 100 feet (30 m) long. They eat other worms, clams, and snails. Most mudflat life is much smaller. Some are too small to see. Tiny **bacteria**, **plankton**, and algae live in the mud.

In the Water

Many forms of life are found in estuary waters. Plankton and algae drift in open water. Large plants, like kelp and sea grass, grow in shallow waters. These plants make food from the sunlight's energy. This is called photosynthesis.

Manatees eat sea grass and algae. These huge, slow mammals can grow to be 13 feet (4 m) long. Young sea turtles cruise through estuary waters. They munch on sea grass, too. They also look for snacks of crabs and snails.

Young fish grow bigger in estuary waters. Some become strong for longer voyages in the open ocean. Salmon, eels, and striped bass all swim in estuaries. They eat smaller fish, worms, and snails. Sharks hunt the larger fish.

Scientists put animals into groups based on what they eat. Manatees are herbivores. They only eat plants. Most sea turtles are omnivores. They eat both plants and animals. Sharks are carnivores. They only eat meat.

The large manatee eats grasses and other plants.

At the Oyster Reef

Oysters are made to live in estuary water. These mollusks close their shells when the tide goes out. Oysters open back up when the tide comes in.

An oyster reef is above water during low tide.

They pull algae and plankton from the water for food. Oysters help keep estuaries clean.

Oysters form huge colonies. First a group of young oysters settles down in one place. The oysters grow old and die. New oysters attach to their shells. The pile of shells keeps growing. Soon a **reef** forms. Some reefs are made from thousands of oysters and oyster shells.

Oyster reefs are important habitats. Sponges, barnacles, and urchins cling to the reefs. Snails, clams, and crabs move in. Fish eat these animals. Rays prowl the reef. They hunt for oysters and clams.

Oysters are a popular food for humans. People have fished and taken too many oysters in some places. This hurts the plants and animals that depend on the oyster shells for their habitat.

The Estuary Food Chain

Many plants and animals live, hunt, and grow in the estuary biome. Each is an important part of an estuary's food chain. This is the way that plants and animals work together in a habitat.

Most food chains begin with sunlight. Estuary plants use the sun's energy to make food. Small animals eat these plants. Fish eat the small animals. Raccoons, water birds, and other larger animals eat the fish.

Every part of an estuary's food chain is important. The whole estuary could be in trouble if just one plant or animal disappeared. We must protect the estuary biome.

Sun

Algae

Shrimp

Shark

In one kind of estuary food chain, sharks eat shrimp,
shrimp eat algae, and algae use sunlight to make food.

GLOSSARY

adapt (uh-DAPT) To adapt is to change slowly over years and years to better fit into a habitat. Fish adapt to the changing water in an estuary.

bacteria (bak-TEER-ee-uh) Bacteria are tiny one-celled living creatures that live all over the earth. Oysters clean bacteria from estuary water.

brackish (BRAK-ish) Brackish water is a mix between salt and freshwater. Brackish water is found along the coasts.

crustaceans (kruh-STAY-shuhnz) Crustaceans are creatures with hard outer skeletons that usually live in or near water. Fiddler crabs are crustaceans that live in estuaries.

delta (DEL-tuh) A delta is a triangle-shaped piece of land where a river enters an ocean. An estuary often forms near a river delta.

habitats (HAB-i-tats) The environments where animals usually live are their habitats. Oyster reefs are important habitats for other animals.

mollusks (MAHL-luhskz) Mollusks are animals with soft bodies and hard shells that live in or near water. Clams and oysters are mollusks that live in estuaries.

plankton (PLANGK-ton) Plankton are tiny plants and animals that drift in water. Many larger estuary animals eat plankton.

predators (PRED-uh-turz) Predators are animals that hunt other animals for food. Sharks and rays are predators.

prey (PRAY) Prey are animals that are hunted for food by other animals. Clams are prey for Alaskan grizzly bears.

reef (REEF) A reef is a strip of rocks, coral, or oyster shells that are near the ocean's surface. Oysters can form a large reef in an estuary.

siphon (SYE-fuhn) A siphon is a tube-like organ that an animal can use to draw in and give out fluids. A clam uses its siphon to eat and breathe.

TO LEARN MORE

BOOKS

Collard, Sneed B. *Many Biomes, One Earth*. Watertown, MA: Charlesbridge, 2009.

Kalman, Bobbie. *The Life Cycle of Salmon*. New York: Crabtree, 2003.

Kurtz, Kevin. *A Day in the Salt Marsh*. Mount Pleasant, SC: Sylvan Dell, 2007.

WEB SITES
Visit our Web site for links about the estuary biome:
childsworld.com/links

Note to Parents, Teachers, and Librarians: We routinely verify our Web links to make sure they are safe and active sites. So encourage your readers to check them out!

INDEX